THOUGHTFULNESS THINKING
Self-Awareness
I0816496
VICKY BUREAU
M.S., SCHOOL COUNSELING
A Starfish Book
SEAHORSE
PUBLISHING

Teaching Tips for Caregivers:

As a caregiver, you can help your child succeed in school by giving them a strong foundation in language and literacy skills and a desire to learn to read.

This book helps children grow by letting them practice reading skills.

Reading for pleasure and interest will help your child to develop reading skills and will give your child the opportunity to practice these skills in meaningful ways.

- Encourage your child to read on her own at home
- Encourage your child to practice reading aloud
- Encourage activities that require reading
- Establish a reading time
- Talk with your child
- Give your child writing materials

Teaching Tips for Teachers:

Research shows that one of the best ways for students to learn a new topic is to read about it.

Before Reading

- Read the "Words to Know" and discuss the meaning of each word.
- Read the back cover to see what the book is about.

During Reading

- When a student gets to a word that is unknown, ask them to look at the rest of the sentence to find clues to help with the meaning of the unknown word.
- Ask the student to write down any pages of the book that were confusing to them.

After Reading

- Discuss the main idea of the book.
- Ask students to give one detail that they learned in the book by showing a text dependent answer from the book.

TABLE OF CONTENTS

Self-Awareness: Do You Have It?

Imagine someone asked you, "What do others think about you?"

What would you say?

Do you know and **understand** who you are?

Sometimes, we feel like we don’t fit in.

We may not understand who we are or **appreciate** what makes us special.

Self-awareness is like a mirror.

You see yourself in the reflection.

But you should see others in there, too!

In other words, to truly see yourself, you need to understand how others see you, too.

There are two parts of self-awareness: self and awareness.

Sounds pretty simple, right?

Self-Awareness: What Does It Mean?

Do you understand yourself?

Do you feel like others understand you?

Having self-awareness means you understand how others see you.

When you look in the mirror, what do you see?

Who's looking back at you?

Being self-aware means that you understand how you make others feel.

You show **empathy** by also understanding how they feel and why they feel that way.

What makes you feel special?

Look within YOU!

Self-Awareness: How Can You Build Yours?

You can learn more about yourself!

Want to know how? Ask yourself, "What makes me...

...ME?"

Think about what others would say or think about you.

What are some good things they could say?

Understanding who you are, and understanding the **role** you play in who other people are, is what helps you become self-aware!

What Would You Do?

You feel **misunderstood** by a classmate. Do you talk to her about how you make her feel?

You draw a self-portrait for a school project. How would others describe your work?

Let's review your answers!

Feeling misunderstood can be frustrating. But, by talking to others about how you make them feel, you are building your self-awareness!

Making a self-portrait is a fun way to explore your self-awareness! Does your portrait match what others would draw?

Words to Know

appreciate (uh-PREE-shee-ate): to understand the value of something

empathy (EM-puh-thee): the ability to feel someone else's emotions

misunderstood (mis-uhn-dur-STOOD): not understood or understood incorrectly

role (rohl): the job, purpose, or part someone plays in a particular situation

self-awareness (self uh-WARE-nuhs): understanding who you are and how that influences others

understand (uhn-duhr-STAND): to grasp the meaning of something

Index

Comprehension Questions

1. How can you show self-awareness?

2. What are some things you can do to build your self-awareness?

3. How does empathy affect self-awareness?

4. What is the difference between understanding and empathy?

About the Author

Vicky Bureau was born in Longueuil, Quebec, and was raised in South Florida. As a teacher, she developed a passion for the social and emotional growth of her students and later transitioned into the area of child and adolescent psychology after earning her master's degree in school counseling.
In addition to working with children, Vicky loves to be surrounded by animals and nature. She lives in Fort Lauderdale with her family: Billy, Khloe, M.J., and Max; her three cats, Alley, Baguette, and Salem; and her dog, Boomer.

Written by: Vicky Bureau
Design by: Under the Oaks Media
Editor: Kim Thompson

Photographs/Shutterstock: Benjavisa Rvangvaree: cover, p. 1; Monkey Business Images: p. 5, 16a, 16b; Kung Min Ju: p. 6; Da Antipana: p. 7; JR-50: p. 8; lassadesign: p. 9; ESB Professional: p. 10-11, 13; Ivanova Ksenia: p. 14; Erica Finstad: p. 17a; Inside Creative House: p. 17b; spass: p. 17c; KlingSup: p. 19

Library of Congress PCN Data
Self-Awareness / Vicky Bureau
Thoughtfulness Thinking
ISBN 978-1-63897-091-0 (hard cover)
ISBN 978-1-63897-177-1 (paperback)
ISBN 978-1-63897-263-1 (EPUB)
ISBN 978-1-63897-349-2 (eBook)
Library of Congress Control Number: 2021945202

Printed in the United States of America.

Seahorse Publishing Company
www.seahorsepub.com

Published in the United States
Seahorse Publishing
PO Box 771325
Coral Springs, FL 33077